Seriously Funny

Book 1

Second Edition

By A Pratt

Copyright ©2021 A Pratt

These jokes have been compiled from various sources both online and offline. Unfortunately I have been unable to find the original source of these jokes. The vast majority are based on content that is freely available in the public domain, and have been repeated countless times in various formats. If anyone feels they have a valid claim to the copyright ownership of the roots of any joke contained herein, please contact me with supporting evidence and credit will be given in the next edition.

1. Whenever I have a headache, I take two aspirins and keep away from children, like the bottle says.

2. My wife just told me she wanted another baby.
   I agreed, the one we have now is really annoying.

3. We have a strange custom in our office. The food has names there. Yesterday for example I got a sandwich out of the fridge and its name was "Michael"

4. Telling a girl to calm down works about as well as trying to baptise a cat.

5. My girlfriend isn't talking to me because apparently I ruined her birthday. I'm not sure how I did that – I didn't even know it was her birthday...

6. Today I went for a walk with a beautiful girl.
   Then she noticed me so we went for a run.

7. I went into a pharmacy and asked "what gets rid of Coronavirus?"
    The assistant replied "ammonia cleaner" I said "I'm sorry, I thought you worked here"

8. Today I learned that humans eat more bananas than monkeys,
    I can't remember the last time I ate a monkey.

9. I went through an expensive and painful procedure yesterday, having had my spine and both testicles removed.
    Still, some of the wedding presents were fantastic.

10. 'Mr. Clark, I have reviewed this case very carefully,' the divorce Court Judge said, 'And I've decided to give your wife £775 a week,'
    'That's very fair, your honour,' the husband said. 'And every now and then I'll try to send her a few pounds myself.'

11. When Dad came home he was astonished to see Peter sitting on a horse, writing something. " What on earth are you doing there ?" he asked.

"Well, the teacher told us to write an essay on our favourite animal. That's why I'm here and that's why Rachel's sitting in the goldfish bowl !"

12. Psychiatrist to nurse: Just say we're very busy. Don't keep saying, It's a madhouse in here.

13. Wife: "I've made the chicken soup."
Husband: "Oh, good. I was worried it was for us."

14. Due to freezing conditions in the UK the men's British Naturist Society has seen the size of their members shrink dramatically.

15. A bear walks into a bar and says, "Give me a whiskey and … cola."
"Why the big pause?" asks the bartender.
The bear shrugged. "I'm not sure; I was born with them."

16. If you're tired of waiting at a restaurant, just call their number and ask if they also deliver to table 16.

17. "What's the name of your new dog?" "I don't know. He won't tell."

18. There's a fine line between a numerator and a denominator. Only a fraction of people will find this funny.

19. Today, my son asked, "can I have a book mark?" and I burst into tears.
11 years old and he still doesn't know my name is Brian.

20. I walked in to the kitchen this morning and said to my lovely wife,
"is that coffee I smell ?"
She replied,
"it is and yes you do"

21. My friend keeps saying "cheer up man it could be worse, you could be stuck underground in a hole full of water."
I know he means well.

22. If you ever get onto a plane and recognise a friend called Jack, don't shout 'Hi Jack!'

23. My professor accused me of plagiarizing His words, not mine.

24. I got fired from my job because I kept asking my customers whether they would

prefer "Smoking" or "Non-smoking".
Apparently the correct terms are
"Cremation" and "Burial".

25.   I threw a ball for my dog...
      It's a bit extravagant I know, but it was his
      birthday and he looks great in a dinner
      jacket.

26.   My carbon monoxide detector keeps
      beeping.
      It is starting to give me a headache.

27.   Three conspiracy theorists walk into a bar
      You can't tell me that's just a coincidence.

28.   Go to the pet store and buy birdseed then
      ask the clerk how long will the birds take
      to grow.

29.   My wife ran off with my best friend last
      week.
      I'm sure going to miss him.

30.   Why did the old man fall in the well?
      Because he couldn't see that well.

31. A local barber was arrested for selling drugs. I've been his customer for five years.
I never knew he was a barber.

32. My friend gave me his Epi-Pen as he was dying. It seemed very important to him that I have it.

33. Old people poke me at weddings and tell me "your next"
So I started doing the same thing to them at funerals.

34. Did you know there are no canaries on the Canary Islands? Same as with the Virgin Islands...
No canaries there either.

35. A man approached a local person in a village he was visiting.
"What's the quickest way to York?"
The local scratched his head.
"Are you walking or driving?" he asked the stranger.
"I'm driving."
The local replied "That's the quickest way!"

36. I asked my wife what she wanted for Christmas. She told me "Nothing would make her happier than a diamond necklace" So I bought her nothing.

37. What's the difference between an Indian and an African elephant?
One is an elephant.

38. I went to the doctors recently.
He said: "Don't eat anything fatty"
I said: "Like what, bacon and burgers?"
He said: "No fatty, don't eat anything."

39. Thanks for explaining the word "many" to me, it means a lot.

40. A clown and a little girl walk through a dark forest.
The girl says, "I'm scared!"
The clown replies, "You think you're scared?
I have to walk back alone!

41. I bought my son a puppy for Christmas, but I've just accidentally killed him with my car as I reversed onto the drive.
Oh well, I'll have to look after the puppy myself now.

42. Give a man a fish and you feed him for a day. Teach a man to fish and you get rid of him all weekend...!

43. I thought my wife was joking when she said she was going to leave me because i wouldn't stop singing "I'm a believer" but then I saw her face.

44. My girlfriend's dog died, so I tried to cheer her up by getting her an identical one. It just made her more upset. She screamed at me, "What am I supposed to do with two dead dogs?"

45. My wife just called and told me three of the girls in the office have just received some flowers for Valentine's Day and they are absolutely gorgeous.
I said, that is probably why the received the flowers then.

46. I've had a friends request from quasi modo I don't think I know him but the name rings a bell.

47. My doctor told me today that I was too sweet.

Well, her exact words were, "severely diabetic", but I knew what she meant.

48. Just changed my Facebook name to 'No one' so when I see stupid posts I can click like and it will say 'No one likes this'.

49. Did you know that if you hold your ear up to a stranger's leg…
You can actually hear them say, "What the heck are you doing?"

50. Last year I was miserable and depressed.
This year I turned it all around though.
Now I am depressed and miserable.

51. I don't often tell Dad jokes.
But when I do, he laughs.

52. Wife: honey, can i hold Henry? (their new baby)
Husband: wait until he cries.
Wife: why?
Husband: because i can't find him.

53. My friend said, "My kid refuses to eat fish. What do you think is a good

replacement?"
I said, "Cats. Cats love fish."

54. I called my wife and told her that I'll pick
up pizza and coke on the way back from
work. But it seems she was not happy.
She still regrets letting me name the kids.

55. Thank you student loans for getting me
through college. I don't think I can ever
repay you.

56. I remember when plastic surgery was a
taboo subject.
Now when you mention Botox, no one
raises an eyebrow.

57. My daughter thinks I don't respect her
personal boundaries
Or at least that's what she wrote in her
diary.

58. PUPIL: "Would you punish me for
something I didn't do?"
TEACHER: "Of course not."
PUPIL:"Good, because I haven't done my
homework."

59. Window Problems A blonde texts her husband on a cold winter's morning: "Windows frozen, won't open." Husband texts back: "Gently pour some lukewarm water over it and gently tap edges with hammer." Wife texts back 5 minutes later: "Computer really messed up now."

60. I just discovered that the word "nothing" i s a palindrome...
Backwards it spells "gnihton", which also means nothing.

61. A couple was going out for the evening. The last thing they did was to put the cat out.
The taxi arrived, and as the couple walked out of the house, the cat shoots back in. So the husband goes back inside to chase it out.
The wife, not wanting it known that the house would be empty, explained to the taxi driver "He's just going upstairs to say goodbye to my mother."
A few minutes later, the husband got into the taxi and said, "Sorry I took so long, the stupid thing was hiding under the bed and I had to poke her with a coat hanger to get her to come out!"

62. What happens when a computer thinks it knows better than a human? Ask Boeing

63. My wife and I share a sense of humour. We have to. She doesn't have one.

64. My wife was drunk one night and told me that I could tie her up and do anything I wanted.
So I tied her up and went fishing.

65. How Long Is A Chinese Name.
No seriously, it is.

66. I achieved my personal best in the 100 metres yesterday...
74 metres.

67. What is easier to pick up the heavier they get?
Women.

68. Mahatma Gandhi, as you know, walked barefoot most of the time, which produced an impressive set of calluses on his feet. He also ate very little, which made him rather frail and with his odd diet, he suffered from bad breath.
This made him... A super callused fragile mystic plagued with halitosis.

69. I'm sure my wife has been putting glue on my weapons collection.
She denies it, but I'm sticking to my guns.

70. Did anyone notice that the "&"symbol looks like a dog dragging his butt across the floor?

71. Just got a wardrobe delivered from IKEA.
Not a single bracket, hinge, screw or dowel.
Seriously, you couldn't make it up.

72. My therapist said I should identify the people in my life that have hurt me, write letters to them explaining what they did and then burn them.
I feel so much better now, but I don't know what to do with all these letters.

73. Wife: 'Darling, look. I haven't worn this in 8 years and it still fits.'
Husband: For God's sake.
It's a scarf!

74. Finland have just closed their borders.
Which means no one can cross the finish line.

75. I own a chewed pencil that Shakespeare once used to write his famous works. He chewed on it so much that I can't tell whether it's 2B or not 2B.

76. I asked my wife to dress up as a nurse tonight to fulfil my fantasy that we have healthcare.

77. The worst time to have a heart attack is during a game of charades.

78. What's the difference between America and a bottle of milk? — In 200 years the milk will have developed a culture.

79. Give a man a fish, and he eats for a day. Teach a Nigerian to phish and he'll become a prince.

80. Two guys were discussing popular family trends on sex, marriage, and family values. Stuart said, 'I didn't sleep with my wife before we got married, did you?'
Leroy replied, 'I'm not sure, what was her maiden name?'

81. 90% of women don't like men in pink shirts. Ironically, 90% of men in pink shirts don't like women.

82. Life after death does exist!
Just not for the person that died.

83. My goal was to lose 15 pounds this month. Only 20 more to go!

84. I scared my postman today by going to the door naked.
I'm not sure what freaked him out more, my naked body or the fact that I knew where he lived.

85. If I ever end up on life support please unplug me.
Then plug me back in again, see if that works.

86. One day you're the best thing since sliced bread. The next, you're toast.

87. I don't approve of political jokes...I've seen too many of them get elected.

88. What's a pirate's least favourite letter?
Dear Sir or Madam,
Your IP address has been flagged for illegally downloading movies. We will have to suspend your account, pending further investigation.
Sincerely,
Your Internet Provider

89. I won $10 million on the lottery this weekend so I decided to donate a quarter of it to charity.
Now I have $9,999,999.75.

90. Little five year old Johnny was in the bath tub, and his mom was washing his hair. She said to him, "Wow, your hair is growing so fast! You need a haircut again." Little Johnny replied, "Maybe you should stop watering it so much."

91. How can you tell your girlfriend is getting fat?
She fits in your wife's clothes.

92. My Doc asked if I drank to excess,
I said I'd drink to anything.

93. My wife caught me cross-dressing and said it's over.
So I packed her things and left.

94. Why are soldiers so tired on 1 April?
Because they just had a 31-day March.

95. A kid asks his mom: "Mom, what is dark humour?"
She responds: "See that boy over there with no arms? Tell him to clap."
The kid replies: "but mom, I'm blind!"
Mom: "Exactly"

96. What's the difference between a religion and a cult?
In a cult, there is someone on top that knows it's all nonsense.
In a religion that person is dead.

97. Any married man should forget his mistakes, there's no use in two people remembering the same thing.

98. Can't believe it's been a year since I didn't become a better person.

99. My wife crashed the car again today. She told the police the man she hit with was on his phone and drinking a beer.
The police said the man can do whatever he wants in his own living room.

100. I picked up a hitchhiker last night. He said thanks how do you know I'm not a serial killer?
I replied the chances of two serial killers being in the same car are astronomical.

101. Just bumped into a mannequin & said "sorry".
Then said "Oh I thought you were a person".
Then realised I was still talking to a mannequin

102. Ever think you'd like to buy a Parrot and teach it to say,
"Help, they've turned me into a parrot"?

103. "I'm sorry" and "I apologize" usually mean the same thing, but not at a funeral.

104. A wife is told by her doctor that she has only 12 hours to live.
So she and her husband decide to spend

their last night together wining and dining.
She says, "Darling, have another brandy"
He says "No I won't thank you"
She says, "Please have another brandy,
we're enjoying ourselves"
He says, "No! It's all right for you, you
haven't got to get up in the morning"

105. They really should stock ATM's better.
I went to 5 different ones today and they
all said insufficient funds.

106. A man goes into a pet shop and says I'd
like to buy a bee, the pet shop owner says
I'm sorry I don't sell bee's the man says
well you've got one in the window.

107. If toast always lands butter-side down,
and cats always land on their feet, what
happens if you strap toast onto the back
of a cat and drop it?

108. A young man agreed to baby-sit one night
so a single mother could have an evening
out. At bedtime he sent the youngsters
upstairs to bed and settled down to watch
football.
One child kept creeping down the stairs,
but the young man kept sending him back

to bed.

At 9pm the doorbell rang, it was the next-door neighbour, Mrs. Brown, asking whether her son was there. The young man brusquely replied, "No."

Just then a little head appeared over the banister and shouted, "I'm here, Mom, but he won't let me go home!"

109. It takes a lot of balls to play golf the way I do.

110. My wife has evil lessons with Satan every week.
I don't know how much she charges.

111. I wanted to grow my own food, but I couldn't find bacon seeds anywhere.

112. I went on a once in a lifetime holiday.
Never again.

113. The word 'Diputseromneve' may look ridiculous,
But backwards it's even more stupid.

114. I was going to give him a nasty look, but he already had one.

115. My boss hates it when I shorten his name to "Dick".
Especially since his name is "Steve".

116. How do you get a philosophy major off of your front porch?
Pay him for the pizza.

117. My wife said she would rather commit suicide than have dementia.
She would never want to place that burden on me.
I said, honey that's the tenth time you've said that.

118. My 14-year-old daughter has finally met her online boyfriend in real life.
It must be true love, I haven't seen her for weeks.

119. Letting the cat out of the bag is a whole lot easier than putting it back in.

120. What's the difference between a school and a ISIS military base? Don't ask me I only fly the drone...

121. Facebook should add a 'WHO CARES' button next to the 'LIKE' button.

122. I still remember when my mom used to tuck me in as a kid.
Man she really wanted a daughter.

123. Every morning is the dawn of a new error.

124. My Chinese waiter thinks all white people look alike and gave my food to the wrong customer
Wait.
Never mind. That wasn't my waiter.

125. I change my car horn to a gunshot sound. People move out of the way a lot faster now.

126. Did you know there are no canaries on the Canary Islands? Same as with the Virgin Islands...
No canaries there either.

127. At the age of 60 my grandpa started walking five miles a day.
He turns 72 tomorrow and we have no idea where he is.

128. My friend Dave drowned in a boating accident, we placed a life jacket on his coffin.
It's what he would have wanted.

129. Employer: "We need someone responsible for the job."
"Sir your search ends here! In my previous job whenever something went wrong, everybody said I was responsible."

130. I was sitting next to my girlfriend when I said, "I love you."
She said, "Is that you or the beer talking?"
I said, "It's me talking to the beer."

131. If you think the way to a man's heart is through his stomach you're aiming too high.

132. Veganism is like Communism.
They are both fine, unless you like food.

133. A college professor asks all of his students to brainstorm and yell out different kinds of stereotypes.
"All blonde girls are dumb!", shouts a guy in the back of the class.
"Sony!", yells the blonde girl in the front.

134. "Well, I've got good news and bad news."
"Give me the good news first, Doc."
"They're going to name a disease after you."

135. A dyslexic insomniac stays awake all night wondering if there really is a dog.

136. If corn oil is made from corn, and vegetable oil is made from vegetables, then what is baby oil made from?

137. Hey dad, how do you feel about abortion?
"Ask your sister"
I don't have a...

138. The book on chronology that I ordered has finally arrived. It's about time.....

139. Why isn't there mouse flavoured cat food?

140. My friend claims that he "accidentally" glued himself to his autobiography, but I don't believe him.
But that's his story, and he's sticking to it.

141. I just lost my job as a zookeeper.
In my defence there were signs

everywhere saying "please don't feed the animals".

142. My mother-in-law fell down a wishing well, I was amazed, I never knew they worked.

143. If you try to fail, and succeed, which have you done?

144. When Susan's boyfriend proposed she said: "I love the simple things in life, but I don't want one of them as a husband".

145. I haven't slept for three days, because that would be too long.

146. Girl: You would be a good dancer except for two things.
Boy: What are the two things?
Girl: Your feet.

147. Why are birthday's good for you?
Statistics show that the people who have the most live the longest!

148. A 3 years old boy sits near a pregnant woman.

Boy: "Why do you look so fat?"

Pregnant woman: "I have a baby inside me".

Boy: "Is it a good baby?"

Pregnant woman: "Yes, it is a very good baby".

Boy: "Then why did you eat it?"

149. My grandfather killed over 30 German pilots in World War II.
He was the worst mechanic in the Luftwaffe.

150. Son: Dad, what's it like to have a handsome son?
Dad: I don't know, ask your grandpa.

151. I recently swapped all the labels on my wife's spice rack, she hasn't noticed yet
But the thyme is cumin.

152. I couldn't afford to take the kids to Sea World.
So I took them to the fish market and said, "shh they are sleeping".

153. Ever think you'd like to buy a Parrot and teach it to say,
"Help, they've turned me into a parrot"?

154. I have a joke about a broken compass.
I'm not sure where I am going with this.

155. You should never take a sleeping pill and a laxative at the same time.
But if you do, you will sleep like a baby.

156. Patient: "Doctor, my wife thinks I'm crazy because I like sausages."
Psychiatrist: "Nonsense! I like sausages too."
Patient: "Good, you should come and see my collection. I've got hundreds of them."

157. My wife is fed up of my constant Dad jokes, so I asked her, "How can I stop my addiction?"
Wife: whatever means necessary.
Me: No it doesn't.

158. An executive was in quandary. He had to get rid of one of his staff.
He had narrowed it down to one of two people, Debra or Jack. It would be a hard decision to make, as they were both equally qualified and both did excellent work.
He finally decided that in the morning whichever one used the water cooler first

would have to go.

Debra came in the next morning, hugely hung-over after partying all night. She went to the cooler to get some water to take an aspirin and the executive approached her and said: "Debra, I've never done this before, but I have to lay you or Jack off."

Debra replied, "Could you jack off, I have a terrible headache."

159. My mom never saw the irony in calling me a son-of-a-bitch.

160. What word is always spelled wrong in the dictionary?
Wrong.

161. My boss pulled up to work in his sweet new Mercedes this morning and I complimented him on it.
He replied: "Well, if you work hard, set goals, stay determined and put in long hours, I can get an even better one next year".

162. If practice makes perfect, and nobody's perfect, why practice?

163. Went to the pub with my girlfriend last night. Locals were shouting "paedophile!" and other names at me, just because my girlfriend is 21 and I'm 50.
It completely spoiled our 10th anniversary.

164. The other day I told a girl, "You look great without glasses."
Girl: "I don't wear glasses."
Me, while polishing my lenses: "No, but I do."

165. I always feel better when my doctor says something is normal for my age but then I think dying will also be normal for my age at some point.

166. Call it a hunch, but I'm pretty sure I have an abnormal convex curvature of the upper spine.

167. A woman has twins, and gives them up for adoption. One of them goes to a family in Egypt and is named 'Amal.' The other goes to a family in Spain, they name him Juan'. Years later; Juan sends a picture of himself to his mum. Upon receiving the picture, she tells her husband that she wished she also had a picture of Amal. Her husband

responds, "But they are twins. If you've seen Juan, you've seen Amal."

168. Remember the 7 qualities for the perfect girlfriend...
Beautiful, Intelligent, Gentle, Thoughtful, Innocent, Trustworthy, Sensible.
Or in other words........... B.I.G.T.I.T.S.

169. And the lord said unto John, "Come forth and you will receive eternal life". John came fifth and won a toaster.

170. The thing I love most about this hot weather is the short skirts and low cut tops.... although, they do make me look a bit gay.

171. "My therapist says I have a preoccupation with vengeance. We'll see about that."

172. I went down the local supermarket, I said, "I want to make a complaint, this vinegar's got lumps in it", he said, "Those are pickled onions"

173. To this day, the boy that used to bully me at school still takes my lunch money.

On the plus side, he makes great Subway sandwiches.

174. If I had a dollar for every time I thought about my wife.
     I'd probably start thinking about her.

175. Just been to the gym. They've got a new machine in. Only used it for half an hour, as I started to feel sick. It's great though. It does everything -KitKats, Mars Bars, Snickers, Potato Crisps, the lot.."

176. 5/4 of people admit that they're bad with fractions.

177. I rang up British Telecom, I said, "I want to report a nuisance caller", he said "Not you again".

178. What did the bald guy say when he was given a comb for his birthday?
     Thanks, I'll never part with it.

179. Hi, I'm Buzz Aldrin. Second person to step on the moon.
     Neil before me.

180. A doctor is the only man who can tell a woman to take off all her clothes and then send a bill to her husband!

181. My grandfather died because a medical report said he had Type-A blood. Unfortunately it was a Type-O.

182. A woman yelled at me yesterday for sleeping on the bus.
Do you know how exhausting it is being a bus driver?

183. I joined the gym and asked trainer, "I want to impress beautiful girls, which machine should I use?"
He said, "The ATM machine"

184. I was walking passed a farm and a sign said "Duck, eggs". I thought, that's an unnecessary comma. And then it hit me.

185. The last thing my grandfather said before he died was "It's worth it to spend money on good speakers."
That was some sound advice.

186. I'm developing a new fragrance for introverts:
Leave me the Fu Cologne.

187. When everything's coming your way, you're in the wrong lane.

188. Time is what keeps things from happening all at once.

189. A recent study has found that women who carry a little extra weight live longer than the men who mention it.

190. A young kid is sitting on a park bench eating a chocolate bar.
The man sitting next to him looks over and says, "Eating too much chocolate is bad for you."
The boy looks over and responds, "My great grandfather lived to be one hundred and one years old".
The man replies, "And he ate as much chocolate as you?"
"No" says the boy, "He minded his own damn business.

191. When tempted to fight fire with fire, remember that the Fire Department usually uses water.

192. When I was applying for Australian citizenship the interviewer asked, "Do you have a criminal record?"
I said, "No. Is that still required?"

193. Mark called in to see his friend Angus (a Scotsman) to find he was stripping the wallpaper from the walls. Rather obviously, he remarked "You're decorating, I see." to which Angus replied "No. I'm moving house."

194. My friend says to me: "What rhymes with orange" I said: "No it doesn't"

195. If you think it's hard to meet new people, pick up the wrong ball on a golf course.

196. I was watching the London Marathon and saw one runner dressed as a chicken and another runner dressed as an egg.
I thought: 'This could be interesting.'

197. PUPIL: "Would you punish me for something I didn't do?"
TEACHER: "Of course not."
PUPIL:"Good, because I haven't done my homework."

198. I found a rock which measured 1760 yards in length.
Must be some kind of milestone.

199. Most people are shocked when they find out how bad an electrician I am.

200. Hedgehogs - why can't they just share the hedge?

201. I'm always frank with my sexual partners. Don't want them knowing my real name, do I?

202. What's the definition of an accountant? Someone who solves a problem you didn't know you had in a way you don't understand.

203. My girlfriend says I have a body of a man half my age, which would be a nice compliment if I wasn't 22.

204. Many things can be preserved in alcohol.
Dignity is not one of them.

205. I've got the best wife in England.
The other one's in Africa!

206. A man is driving down a highway in his
Ferrari when he is pulled over by cop!
The driver says: Officer why did you pull
me over?
The cop says: For speeding!
The driver says: Why officer I saw a sign
back there that said 90!
The cop says: That is the road number sir!
The driver says: Thank God you didn't pull
me over on highway 181!!!

207. Teacher: "This essay on your dog is, word
for word, the same as your brother's."
Student: Yes, sir, it is the same dog."

208. Two cows are standing in a field. One cow
says "Did you hear about that outbreak of
mad cow disease? It makes cows go
completely insane!". The other cow replies
"Good thing I'm a helicopter".

209. Who says nothing is impossible.
I've been doing nothing for years.

210. Why do married men gain weight and bachelors don't?
The bachelors go to the refrigerator, see nothing they want, then go to bed.
Married guys go to bed, see nothing they want, then go to the refrigerator.

211. A horse walks into a bar and the bartender says, "Sir, why the long face."

212. A woman gets on a bus with her baby. The driver says, "Ugh! That's the ugliest baby I've ever seen."
The woman stalks off to the rear of the bus and sits down. She turns to the man sitting next to her and says, "The driver just insulted me!"
The man says, "You go and give him a telling off. I'll hold your monkey for you."

213. A man says to his new girlfriend:
"Since I first laid eyes on you, I've wanted to make love to you really badly."
"Well," she replies, "You succeeded."

214. Right now I'm having amnesia and deja vu at the same time! I think I've forgotten this before?

215. Where do they get the seeds to plant seedless watermelons?

216. Marriage is the main reason for divorce.

217. I told my Dad to embrace his mistakes. He started to tear up and gave me a hug.

218. If I had to use one word to describe myself it would be bad at following directions.

219. A bank robber pulls out gun points it at the teller, and says, "Give me all the money or you're geography!" The puzzled teller replies, "Did you to say history?". The bank robber says, "Don't change the subject!".

220. I called the Suicide Hotline in Iraq. They were very excited and wanted to know if I could drive a truck.

221. Truck driver is stuck under bridge. Cars are backed up for miles. Finally, a police car comes up. The cop gets out of his car and walks around to the truck driver, puts his hands on his hips and says, "Got stuck, huh?"

The truck driver says, "No, I was delivering this bridge and ran out of gas."

222. Justice is a dish best served cold
If it were served warm it would be justwater.

223. My grandpa always used to say "as one door closes, another opens". A lovely man. A terrible cabinet maker.

224. Two aerials meet on a roof, they fall in love and get married. The ceremony wasn't much but the reception was brilliant.

225. Two cannibals are eating a clown. One says to the other "Does this taste funny to you?"

226. If God didn't want us to eat animals, he wouldn't have made them out of food.

227. What does the word minimum mean?
A small mother.

228. The pen is mightier than the sword and considerably easier to write with.

229. Everybody thought Anybody could do it, but Nobody realised that Everybody wouldn't do it.
It ended up that Everybody blamed Somebody for what Anybody could have done.

230. What's black and white and eats like a horse.
A Zebra.

231. A man says to his buddy, "My wife talks to herself".
His buddy says, "Don't worry, my wife has been doing that for years, she just thinks I am listening".

232. Whenever I find the key to success, someone changes the lock.

233. I just let my mind wander, and it didn't come back.

234. Marriage is a great institution... but who wants to live in an institution?

235. A man takes his dog for a walk in the park. While he's there, he runs in to his old

friend.

The two men stop to talk and the dog just plops right down and starts licking his balls.

The friend sees this and says, "Man, I sure wish I could do that."

The dog owner says, "Go ahead, but pet him a little bit first."

236. Teacher asked George: "How can you prove the earth is round?"

George replied: "I can't. Besides, I never said it was."

237. What did the Buddhist say to the hot dog vendor?

Make me one with everything.

The hot dog vendor then gives him the dog and the Buddhist gives him a $20.

Buddhist – Hey, where's my change?

Vendor – Change must come from within.

238. It's a five minute walk from my house to the pub.

It's a thirty five minute walk from the pub to my house.

The difference is staggering.

239. What is the most popular Christmas wine?
"I don't like Brussels Sprouts".

240. Don't you hate it when people answer
their own questions?
I know I do.

241. My friends told me I'd never be good at
poetry because I'm dyslexic.
They couldn't be more wrong, so far I've
made three jugs and a vase.

242. What if there were no hypothetical
questions?

243. Have you ever tried blindfolded archery?
You don't know what you're missing!

244. The fact that there is a highway to hell and
a stairway to heaven says a lot about the
anticipated traffic load.

245. Has anyone actually heard a wolf whistle?

246. I read today about the dangers of drinking.
It really scared me. So after today, no
more reading!

247. How can a spokesman make no comment?

248. My Dad used to say 'always fight fire with fire', which is probably why he got thrown out of the fire brigade.

249. What do you call a boomerang that doesn't work?
A stick.

250. Is this insecticide good for beetles. - No, it'll kill them!

251. How do you stop a fish from smelling?
Cut its nose off.

252. Why can't your nose be 12 inches long?
Cause then it would be a foot!

253. A thief stuck a pistol in a man's ribs and said, "Give me your money." The gentleman, shocked by the sudden attack, said "You cannot do this, I'm a United States congressman!" The thief said, "In that case, give me my money!"

254. I totally understand how batteries feel because I'm rarely ever included in things either.

255. Yesterday at the gym I asked a girl what her new year's resolution was.
She said "Screw you".
So I'm pretty excited for the new year.

256. No matter how kind you are, German children are kinder.

257. Why is every gender equality officer female?
Because it is cheaper.

258. Why don't you ever see hippopotamus hiding in trees?
Because they're really good at it.

259. When would an Aussie cricketer have 100 runs against his name?
When he is bowling.

260. Dentists make money off of people with bad teeth.
Why should I trust the toothpaste they recommend?

261.   Did you hear about the florist who had
       two kids?
       One's a budding genius and the other is a
       blooming idiot.

262.   A boy with a monkey on his shoulder was
       walking down the road when he passed a
       policeman who said, "Now, now young
       lad, I think you had better take that
       monkey to the zoo."
       The next day, the boy was walking down
       the road with the monkey on his shoulder
       again, when he passed the same
       policeman.
       The policeman said, "Hey there, I thought I
       told you to take that money to the zoo!"
       The boy answered, "I did! Today I'm taking
       him to the cinema."

263.   I met a nice girl at a bar last night and
       asked her to call me when she made it
       home.
       She must be homeless.

264.   I went to the gym earlier and jumped on
       the treadmill.
       People were giving me funny looks so I
       started jogging instead.

265. A man walked into the doctors,
The doctor said " I haven't seen you in a long time "
The man replied "I know I've been ill"

266. A young lady is walking along a river embankment enjoying the spring day and looks up and down the river to see where she can cross. There is another young lady walking along on the other side and asks, "How do I get on the other side". The girl looks up and down the river then replies, "You are on the other side.

267. I've developed an irrational fear of escalators.
I always find myself taking steps to avoid them.

268. Parents: We just donated all of your toys to the orphanage.
Child: Why did you do that?
Parents: We don't want you to be bored.

269. Teacher to Johnny: "Wake up, Johnny! You can't sleep in class!"
Johnny to teacher: "I could actually, it's just that you're a bit loud."

270. My wife sent her photograph to the Lonely Hearts Club.
They sent it back saying they weren't that lonely.

271. It turns out my high school Chemistry teacher was right after all.
Alcohol is a solution.

272. Why are women and children evacuated first in an emergency?
So grown men can try to solve the problem in peace.

273. I told my doctor that I broke my arm in two places.
He told me to stop going to those places.

274. When I see a woman driving a bus I smile and think about how far we as a society have come in equality.
And then I wait for the next bus.

275. What do politicians and diapers have in common?
Both should be changed regularly and for the same reason.

276. I would have asked God for a bike, but I know God doesn't work that way.
So I stole a bike and asked for forgiveness.

277. Wifi went down for five minutes, so i had to talk to my family.
They seem like nice people.

278. Originally I was not going to get a brain transplant.
But then I changed my mind.

279. Patient: The problem is obesity runs in my family.
Doctor: No, the problem is no one in your family runs.

280. Two mice were chewing on an old roll of film when one looks at the other and says, "I think the book was better".

281. Today I found out that my wife is going to divorce me because of my mental illness.
At least that is what the dog keeps telling me.

282. What is the difference between a pregnant woman and a light bulb?
You can unscrew a light bulb

283. Whose cruel idea was it for the word "Lisp" to have an "S" in it?

284. I have kleptomania. But when it gets bad, I take something for it.

285. A man is walking in the desert with his horse and his dog when the dog says, "I can't do this. I need water." The man says, "I didn't know dogs could talk."
The horse says, "Me neither!"

286. Last night my girlfriend and I watched three DVDs back to back.
Luckily I was the one facing the TV.

287. I keep getting the urge to purchase a big white bear from the Arctic.
My doctor says I may have 'Buy Polar' disorder.

288. I just penned a song about a tortilla; actually it's more of a wrap.

289. A woman caught her husband on the bathroom scale sucking in his stomach.
"That doesn't help", she said.
"Yes it does, it is the only way I can see the numbers", he replied.

290. A teenage girl had been talking on the phone for nearly an hour before she hung up. "Wow!," said her father, "That was short. You usually talk for two hours. What happened?"
"Wrong number," she said.

291. Darth Vader had a corrupt brother, Taxi Vader.

292. School children shouldn't be separated according to academic ability; it'll only end in tiers.

293. I bumped into an old school friend at the store today. He started showing off, talking about his well paid job and expensive sports cars.
Then he pulled out his phone and showed me a photo of his wife and said, "She's beautiful, isn't she?"
I said, "If you think she's gorgeous, you should see my girlfriend."

He said, "Why? Is she a stunner?"
I said, "No, she's an optometrist."

294. I'm going to stand outside. So if anyone asks, I am outstanding.

295. A man takes his Rottweiler to the vet.
'My dog's cross-eyed, is there anything you can do for him?'
'Well,' says the vet, 'let's have a look at him'.
So he picks the dog up and examines his eyes, then checks his teeth.
Finally, he says, 'I'm going to have to put him down.'
'What? Because he's cross-eyed?'
'No, because he's really heavy'

296. The police came to my house last night, showing me a picture, asked, "Is this your wife, sir?, I answered, "Yes".
Then they said, "I'm afraid it looks like she's been hit by a bus.", "I know, but she's good with the kids", I replied.

297. In the back woods of Arkansas, Mr. Stewart's wife went into labour in the middle of the night, and the doctor was called out to assist in the delivery. To keep

the nervous father-to-be busy, the doctor handed him a lantern and said, "Here, you hold this high so I can see what I'm doing." Soon, a wee baby boy was brought into the world. "Whoa there Scotty!" said the doctor. "Don't be in a rush to put the lantern down... I think there's yet another wee one to come." Sure enough, within minutes he had delivered another little baby. "No, no, don't be in a great hurry to be putting down that lantern, young man... It seems there's yet another one besides!" cried the doctor. The new father scratched his head in bewilderment, and asked the doctor: "Do ya think it's the light that's attracting' them?"

298. Two hydrogen atoms walk into a bar.
One says, "I've lost my electron."
The other says, "Are you sure?"
The first replies, "Yes, I'm positive..."

299. A man walks in to the doctors surgery with a fried egg on his head.
doctor says why do you have a fried egg on your head.
man replies, the boiled ones keep rolling off.

300. I went to the butchers the other day and I bet him 50 bucks that he couldn't reach the meat off the top shelf.
He said, 'no, the steaks are too high.'

301. I spotted an albino Dalmatian yesterday.
It was the least I could do for him.

302. If you rearrange the letters of MAILMEN
They become VERY ANGRY

303. What's red and bad for your teeth?
A brick.

304. Do you ever notice that when you're driving, anyone going slower than you is an idiot and everyone driving faster than you is a maniac?

305. A grasshopper walks into a bar.
The bartender says "Hey, we've got a drink named after you."
Grasshopper says "You've got a drink named Steve?"

306. A child was continually asking his Mom to buy him a hamster.
When she did, the child looked after it for

a couple of days, but soon he got bored, and it became the Mom's responsibility to feed it.

One day she got upset with the her son's carelessness and asked him, "How many times do you think this hamster would have died until now, if I wasn't looking after it?"

The child replied, "Um, I don't know. Once?"

307.   What kind of horses go out after dusk?
Nightmares!

308.   I still remember what my grandpa said before he kicked the bucket.
He said "how far do you think I can kick this bucket?

309.   Our neighbourhood has a tiny ghost that helps out during hard times.
it's good to have a little community spirit.

310.   I hate people who use big words just to make themselves look perspicacious.

311.   Last night I bought an alcoholic ginger beer,
he wasn't happy about it.

312. What's orange and sounds like a parrot?
A carrot.

313. A woman answered the doorbell with a man standing on her porch. The man said, "I'm terribly sorry. I just ran over your cat and I would like to replace it for you." The woman replied, "Well that's alright with me, but how are you at catching mice?"

314. I tried to start up a chicken dating agency but failed,
it was a struggle to make hens meet.

315. I've invented a new flavour of crisps,
if they're successful I'll make a packet.

316. I've just put my friend Richard on speed dial on the phone,
it's my Get-Rich-Quick scheme.

317. On the first day of school, the teacher asked a student, "What are your parents' names?" The student replied, "My father's name is Laughing and my mother's name is Smiling." The teacher said, "Are you kidding?" The student said, "No, Kidding is my brother. I am Joking."

318. A man has died after falling in a vat of
coffee,
it was instant.

319. How do you get a dog to stop barking in
the front seat?
Put him in the back seat

320. I told my boss I come out in a rash every
time I get my wages,
he asked why,
"because I'm allergic to peanuts".

321. My girlfriend asked me to buy something
that makes her look sexy again, so I got a
crate of lager in.

322. If you feel a bit lonely, forgotten, or just
need someone to cheer you up
remember...You can always change your
birthday on facebook!

323. The human soul weighs 1.2lbs. I know
because I've weighed myself before and
after I walk into my job.

324. People treat me like god.
They ignore my existence until they need something.

325. They say you are what you eat, so lay off the nuts.

326. So what if I can't spell 'Armageddon', it's not like it's the end of the world.

327. A boy is selling fish on a corner. To get his customers' attention, he is yelling, "Dam fish for sale! Get your dam fish here!" A pastor hears this and asks, "Why are you calling them 'dam fish.'" The boy responds, "Because I caught these fish at the local dam." The pastor buys a couple fish, takes them home to his wife, and asks her to cook the dam fish. The wife responds surprised, "I didn't know it was acceptable for a preacher to speak that way." He explains to her why they are dam fish. Later at the dinner table, he asks his son to pass the dam fish. He responds, "That's the spirit, Dad! Now pass the f*cking potatoes!"

328. Why did the scarecrow get promotion? Because he was outstanding in his field.

329. Why can't you hear a pterodactyl urinate?,
because its "P" is silent.

330. My son thinks I set the bar too high for
him as a child.
He never really got over it.

331. My friend was a victim of his own success,
his trophy cabinet fell on him.

332. A man takes his Rottweiler to the vet and
says, "My dog's cross-eyed, is there
anything you can do for him?"
"Well," says the vet, "let's have a look at
him."
So he picks the dog up and examines his
eyes, then checks his teeth. Finally, he
says "I'm going to have to put him down."
"What? Because he's cross-eyed?"
"No, because he's really heavy."

333. Alphabet Spaghetti warning:-
'May contain N, U, T and S'.

334. I got an e-mail saying, 'At Google Earth we
can read maps backwards!',
I thought, "that's just spam."

335. I'm glad I'm not bisexual,
      I couldn't stand being rejected by men as
      well as women.

336. Two athletes arrived at their sleeping
      quarters, before competing in the Olympic
      Games.
      As they exchanged greetings with each
      other, one of the athletes asked the other,
      "So ... are you a pole vaulter?" to which
      came the reply,
      "No! I am a German ... and how do you
      know my name is Valter?"

337. I've been working for an Arab dairy
      farmer or Milk Sheikh as he prefers to be
      called.

338. I used to be a freelance journalist, but I
      was rubbish,
      Lance is still in prison.

339. Don't judge someone until you walk a mile
      in their shoes.
      That way, when you do judge them, you're
      a mile away and you have their shoes.

340. My wife laughed when I said I still had the body of an 18 year old.
Until she checked the freezer.

341. A teacher asked, "Johnny, can you tell me the name of three great kings who have brought happiness and peace into people's lives?" Little Johnny responded, "Drin-king, smo-king, and f*c-king."

342. Do you know what DNA stands for?
National Dyslexic Association

343. Doug Engelbart, the visionary who invented the computer mouse, has died aged 88.
Shame they couldn't right click and save him.

344. A group of young men were sitting around the coffee shop complaining about how hard it was to get by in this day and age. Bob, an old timer, was listening to them and finally spoke. "You kids don't know what hard times are. Why, when I was your age we were so poor we couldn't afford electricity. Why, we even had to watch television by candle light."

345. I Googled- "Missing medieval servant",
it came up with "Page not found"

346. Q: What's the difference between a lentil
and a chickpea?
A: I wouldn't pay $200 to have a lentil on
my face.

347. A little kid was out trick-or-treating on
Halloween dressed as a pirate. He rang a
house's doorbell and the door was opened
by a lady. "Oh, how cute! A little pirate!
And where are your buccaneers?" she
asked. The boy replied, "Under my buckin'
hat."

348. I'm hosting a charity concert for people
who struggle to reach orgasm.
If you can't come, let me know.

349. Did you hear about the poor little fishy
who could not get a loan?
In the end he went to the loan shark.

350. I bought a Teddy Bear the other day for
£5, named it Mohammed and sold it today
for £10.
Does that mean I've made a prophet?

351. Teacher: "Kids, what does the chicken give you?"
Student: "Meat!"
Teacher: "Very good! Now what does the pig give you?"
Student: "Bacon!"
Teacher: "Great! And what does the fat cow give you?"
Student: "Homework!"

352. Youth goes into a bar: Give me a beer, please
Barmaid: You're only 16. Do you want to get me into trouble?
Youth: Later, maybe, but now I just want a beer.

353. You can never lose a homing pigeon - if your homing pigeon doesn't come back what you've lost is a pigeon.

354. Why did the leprechaun wear two condoms?
To be sure, to be sure.

355. A man suggests to his wife, "Darling, shall we try swapping positions tonight."
"That's a great idea," she replies.

"Why don't you stand by the ironing board while I sit on the sofa and break wind."

356. At a cocktail party, one woman says to another, "Aren't you wearing you wedding ring on the wrong finger?"
The other replies, "Yes I am. I married the wrong man."

357. An Irishman, a Chinaman and an American all walk into a bar. This is an excellent example of integrated community.

358. A highway patrolman pulled alongside a speeding car on the freeway. Glancing at the car, he was astounded to see that the blonde behind the wheel was knitting! Realizing that she was oblivious to his flashing lights and siren, the trooper cranked down his window, turned on his bullhorn and yelled, 'PULL OVER!'
'NO!' the blonde yelled back, 'IT'S A SCARF!'

359. The old man hobbled into the doctor's surgery and pleaded,
"Doctor, please help me, you've got to give me something to lower my sex drive."
"Come on now, Mr Bates," replied the

doctor, looking at the doddering old man. "Your sex drive is all in the head."

"That's what I mean. I need something to lower it."

360. What do you call a Deer with no eyes?
No eye-Deer

361. What do you call a Deer with no eyes and no legs?
Still No eye-Deer

362. One day there were three people. Their names were Manners, Trouble and Shut up. One day they were playing hide and seek. Manners got a tummy ache so he went to the toilet. Trouble was hiding. Shut up was finding Trouble when he met a policeman. The policeman said, "What is your name?" "Shut up!" The policeman replied, "Are you looking for trouble?" "Yes!" The policeman fumed, "Where are your manners?" "In the toilet."

363. I left my last girlfriend because she wouldn't stop counting.
I wonder what she's up to now.

364. A woman walked up to the manager of a department store. "Are you hiring any help?" she asked. "No," he said. "We already have all the staff we need." "Then would you mind getting someone to wait on me?" she asked.

365. A man said to me: 'I'm going to attack you with the neck of a guitar.'
I said: 'Is that a fret?'

366. Where there's a will, there's a relative.

367. Crime in multi-storey car parks is wrong on so many different levels.

368. Two nuns are driving down the road when Dracula jumps out.
"Quickly," says the first, "show him your cross".
The other winds down the window, leans out and yells "Get out of the road you goofy ########!"

369. The people of Saudi Arabia don't like the Flintstones but the people of Abu Dhabi do.

370. A little girl became restless as the preacher's sermon dragged on and on. Finally, she leaned over to her mother and whispered, "Mommy, if we give him the money now, will he let us go?

371. What's blue and smells like red paint? Blue paint.

372. What's the difference between light and hard? You can sleep with a light on.

373. How much did the pirate pay to get his ears pierced? A buccaneer.

374. I asked my North Korean friend how it was there, he said he couldn't complain.

375. I refused to believe my road worker father was stealing from his job, but when I got home, all the signs were there.

376. Whiteboards are remarkable.

377. Marriage is the process of finding out what kind of person your spouse would have preferred.

378. I haven't talked to my wife in three weeks. I didn't want to interrupt her.

379. What's ET short for? So he can fit in the spaceship.

380. The first time I got a universal remote control, I thought to myself "This changes everything."

381. What do you get from a pampered cow? Spoiled milk.

382. What's black and white and red all over? A dead zebra.

383. Everyone is gifted, but some people never open their package.

384. A husband and wife were trying to set up a new password to their computer. A husband, "Put 'MYP*NIS' " and the wife fell on the ground laughing cause on

screen was error, "Error. Not long enough."

385. If 4 out of 5 people suffer from diarrhoea; does that mean that one enjoys it?

386. How do you get rid of a cold?
Turn the heating on.

387. Politicians and diapers have one thing in common.
They should both be changed regularly, and for the same reason.

388. "You seem to have more than the average share of intelligence for a man of your background," sneered the lawyer at a witness on the stand.
"If I wasn't under oath, I'd return the compliment," replied the witness.

389. He who laughs last thinks slowest.

390. Why did the monkey fall out of the tree?
Because it was dead.

391. A hungry traveller stops at a monastery and is taken to the kitchens. A brother is

frying chips. 'Are you the friar?' he asks. 'No. I'm the chip monk,' he replies.

392. Wife: Our new neighbour always kisses his wife when he goes to work, why don't you do that?
Husband: How can I? I don't even know her.

393. My girlfriend hates when I make jokes about her weight.
She needs to lighten up.

394. Do you know why you are supposed to bury a politician 100 feet down?
Because deep down they are really good people.

395. My ex was an absolute treasure. By treasure, I mean you will need a map and a shovel to find her.

396. On the other hand, you have different fingers.

397. I owe, I owe, so it's off to work I go.

398. One night, as a couple lays down for bed, the husband starts rubbing his wife's arm. The wife turns over and says "I'm sorry honey, I've got a gynaecologist appointment tomorrow and I want to stay fresh."
The husband, rejected, turns over.
A few minutes later, he rolls back over and taps his wife again.
"Do you have a dentist appointment tomorrow too?"

399. Patient : "Doctor I keep hearing "The green, green grass of home" in my head.
Doctor: "That's called the Tom Jones Syndrome"
Patient: "Is it common?"
Doctor: "It's not unusual"

400. A mushroom walks into a bar. The bartender says to the mushroom. "Hey we don't serve your kind here."
The mushroom says "why not "why not I'm a fun guy"

401. How long did Cain hate his brother?
As long as he was Able.

402. My friend recently got crushed by a pile of books, but he's only got his shelf to blame.

403. What do you call dangerous precipitation? A rain of terror.

404. Atheism is a non-prophet organization.

405. One day I changed a light bulb, crossed the road, and walked into a bar.
That is the day I realized my whole life is a joke.

406. I ordered a chicken and an egg from amazon...
I'll let you know.

407. A suspect is brought into an interrogation room when he says, "I'm not saying a word without my lawyer present".
The cop yells at him, "you are a lawyer".
The man replies, "exactly, so where is my present".

408. What do you call a dinosaur with a extensive vocabulary?
A thesaurus.

409. They all laughed when I said I wanted to be a comedian.
Well, they're not laughing now.

410. Before marriage, a man yearns for the woman he loves. After marriage, the "y" becomes silent.

411. We never knew he was a drunk... until he showed up to work sober.

412. One entrepreneur says to another: "I've just been in the Far East prospecting for gold."
"Japan?" asks the second entrepreneur.
"Gosh, no," he replies. "I used much more scientific methods."

413. A boy asks his father, "Dad, are bugs good to eat?" "That's disgusting. Don't talk about things like that over dinner," the dad replies. After dinner the father asks, "Now, son, what did you want to ask me?" "Oh, nothing," the boy says. "There was a bug in your soup, but now it's gone."

414. Can you believe my neighbour rang my doorbell at 5 am?
Luckily I was already up, playing drums.

415. I don't have a Facebook or Twitter account, so I just go around announcing out loud what I'm doing at random times... I've got 3 followers so far, but I think 2 are cops.

416. I bought a lamp from IKEA the other day. The assistant asked if I was putting it up myself. I said, No, I'm putting it in my lounge.

417. Airline hostesses show you how to use a seat belt in case you haven't been in a car since 1956.

418. "You seem to be in some distress," said the kindly judge to the witness. "Is anything the matter?"
"Well, your Honour," said the witness, "I swore to tell the truth, the whole truth and nothing but the truth, but every time I try, some lawyer objects."

419. My drug test just came back negative. My dealer sure has some explaining to do.

420. When I was six, my family moved to a new city, but fortunately I was able to track them down.

421. Jesus is on Twitter. Mind you he's only got the 12 followers.

422. Doctor: Madam, your husband needs rest and peace so here are some sleeping pills.
      Wife: Doc, when should I give them to him?
      Doctor: They are for you!

423. A lion would never ever cheat on his wife. But a tiger wood.

424. I married Miss Right. I just didn't know her first name was Always.

425. I asked my wife if she wanted to go for a walk today. She said it sounded like a great idea.
      So I told her to pick me up some cigarettes and beer on her way home.

426. A man went into a chemist's shop and said 'Have you got anything for laryngitis?'
      The chemist said 'Good morning sir. What can I do for you?'

427. I phoned the local ramblers club today, and this bloke just went on and on.

428. I have a new theory on inertia but it doesn't seem to be gaining momentum.

429. A Higgs boson walks into a church. The priest says
"Get out, you blasphemer. How dare you call yourself the 'God particle'?"
The Higgs boson replies: "But I make up the mass."

430. How do crazy people go through the forest?
They take the psycho path.

431. A woman has the last word in any argument.
Anything a man says after that is the beginning of a new argument.

432. The last thing I want to do is hurt you... but it's still on the list.

433. What's the difference between a man and a chimpanzee?
One is hairy, smelly and always scratching its arse, and the other is a chimpanzee.

434. One evening, a wife drew her husband's attention to the couple next door and said, "Do you see that couple? How devote they are? He kisses her every time they meet. Why don't you do that?"
"I would love to," replied the husband, "but I don't know her well enough."

435. What belongs to you but others use more? Your name.

436. A wife got so mad at her husband she packed his bags and told him to get out. As he walked to the door she yelled, "I hope you die a long, slow, painful death." He turned around and said, "So, you want me to stay?"

437. If you want to find out who loves you more, stick your wife and dog in the trunk of your car for an hour.
When you open the trunk, who is happy to see you?

438. My boss is going to fire the employee with the worst posture. I have a hunch, it might be me.

439. A guy needed a horse, so he went to a temple and got one.

    Before he left, the priest told him that it was a special horse.

    In order for it to go, he would have to say "Thank God" and for it to stop he would have to say "Amen".

    So the guy rode off, and a few minutes later he dozed off, he woke up and was going off the edge of a cliff.

    So he shouted "Amen!" and the horse stopped a few inches from the edge.

    "Whew," he said. "Thank God."

440. Can a kangaroo jump higher than the Empire State Building?

    Of course. The Empire State Building can't jump.

441. Sometimes it's better to keep your mouth shut and give the impression that you're stupid than open it and remove all doubt.

442. "I was in the restaurant yesterday when I suddenly realized I desperately needed to pass gas.

    The music was really, really loud, so I timed my gas with the beat of the music.

    After a couple of songs, I started to feel

better. I finished my coffee, and noticed
that everybody was staring at me....
Then I suddenly remembered that I was
listening to my iPod."

443.   Two husbands were having a
       conversation, First guy (proudly): "My
       wife's an angel!"
       Second guy: "You're lucky, mine's still
       alive."

444.   How can you go straight on at a
       roundabout?

445.   A boy asked his father, Is it true, Dad, that
       in some parts of Africa a man doesn't
       know his wife until he marries her?
       Dad: That happens in every country, son.

446.   What's the difference between an Indian
       and an African elephant?
       One is an elephant.

447.   At the cocktail party, one woman said to
       another, "Aren't you wearing your
       wedding ring on the wrong finger?"
       The other replied, "Yes I am, I married the
       wrong man."

448. What do you call a man with no body and just a nose?
Nobody nose.

449. Husband: When I get mad at you, you never fight back. How do you control your anger?
Wife: I clean the toilet.
Husband: How does that help?
Wife: I use your Toothbrush.

450. A jumper cable walks into a bar. The bartender says, "I'll serve you, but don't start anything".

451. If your dog is fat you aren't getting enough exercise.

452. Patient - Doctor, doctor! I keep thinking I'm a dog.
Doctor - Take a seat.
Patient - I can't, I'm not allowed on the furniture.

453. I tried to donate some blood yesterday but they asked too many questions.
Like "Who's blood is this?" and "Where did you get it?".

454. Instead of "the John," I call my toilet "the Jim."
That way it sounds better when I say I go to the Jim first thing every morning.

455. I've just started reading a new horror novel written in Braille.
Something really scary is going to happen soon, I can feel it.

456. An old woman goes to the doctors and says, "Doctor, I have this terrible discharge."
The doctor answers, "Take your panties off." So she does, he has a rummage around and says, "How does that feel?"
She answers, "Wonderful, but I came about my ears!"

457. One alien says to another, "The dominant life forms on the planet earth appear to have developed satellite-based nuclear weapons."
The second alien replies, "Are they an emerging intelligence?"
The first alien says, "I don't think so, they have them aimed at themselves."

458. What's the difference between communism and a pencil?
The pencil works on things other than paper.

459. A vegan once said to me, people who sell meat are disgusting.
I replied, people who sell fruits and vegetables are grocer.

460. After you die, what part of your body is the last to stop working?
Your pupils. They dilate.

461. How do you milk a sheep?
Put an apple logo on your product.

462. I tried to share a bag of chips with a homeless person today.
He told me to go away and buy my own.

463. A woman visited her doctor complaining that she hurt all over.
When the doctor asked her to be more specific, she touched her nose, "Ouch!" she cried, and touched her left earlobe, "Arghh!" even that hurts, doctor!"
The doctor checked her over, he then informed her that she had a broken finger.

464. Psychiatrist to his nurse: "Just say we're very busy. Don't keep saying 'It's a madhouse.'"

465. Is Google male or female?
Female, because it doesn't let you finish a sentence before making a suggestion.

466. A Cable repairman was on my street today and he asked me what time it was.
I replied "It is between 1 and 8 pm."

467. Don't you hate it when you can't sleep because you are reminded of a mistake you made 3 years ago?
I hate it when my kid won't stop crying in the middle of the night.

468. Daddy reads some bedtime stories to make little Jonny fall asleep. Half an hour later mommy opens the door quietly and asks: "And, is he asleep?" Little Jonny answers: "Yes, finally."

469. "What do we want?"
"HEARING AIDS!"
"When do we want them?"
"HEARING AIDS!"

470. When the cannibal was late for dinner, he got the cold shoulder.

471. Marriage is like a deck of cards. In the beginning all you need is two hearts and a diamond. By the end you wish you had a club and spade.

472. China should be a baseball team because they can take out the whole world with just a bat

473. I made a website for orphans, unfortunately it doesn't have a homepage.

474. How do Mexicans feel about Trump's wall? – They'll get over it.

475. Will glass coffins be a success? – Remains to be seen.

476. A German went to France for holiday and here is the scene, French border staff: Occupation? German: No, no, no, just visiting.

477. "Hey today was great" "What happened" "I ran into my ex today" "What's so great about that?" "I was in my car"

478. I walked into the kitchen and saw my wife chopping up onions which made me cry.

479. Hi, Welcome to Dave's Orphanage you make them we take them how may I help you?

480. I thought my vasectomy would keep my wife from getting pregnant, but apparently it just changes the colour of the baby.

481. The Somalian Olympics Team has just apologized to the Olympic Committee after realizing that sailing and shooting were two separate events.

482. After my wife died, I couldn't even look at another woman for 10 years. But now that I'm out of jail, I can honestly say it was worth it!

483. Accordion to a recent survey, replacing words with the names of musical

instruments in a sentence often goes undetected.

484. Why did the chicken commit suicide? To get to the other side.

485. When we were visiting the Hoover dam. I started to get a bit hungry. I asked my parents, "Where's the dam snack bar?"

486. What's the best part about twenty eight year olds?
There's twenty of them

487. School shooting happens.
Foreign exchange student: Sobbing under desk
American student: "First time?"

488. Some people think incest jokes are funny. I just think it's all relative.

489. Today someone was killed with a starter pistol. Police think it might be race related.

490. My aunt's star sign was cancer, pretty ironic how she died. – She was eaten by a giant crab.

491. To whoever stole my antidepressants I hope you are happy now.

492. I finally got one of those roof boxes for the car. It's very practical. I can barely hear my kids now.

493. What animal has five legs? - A pitbull returning from a playground.

494. Daddy, there is a man at the door. He says he is collecting for the nursing home. - That's perfect. Tell him grandpa is coming in a moment.

495. My Chinese friend got really sick one day and had to go to a hospital. I went to see him the next day, but he just kept whispering "Chun Yu Yan" over and over – and then died. I was very sad and googled his last message after the burial. Apparently, it means "You're standing on my oxygen tube."

496. Bertie comes sadly to his mommy and says, "Mom, the kids have been mean to me. They keep teasing me that my feet are too big. Please tell me honestly. Are my feet to big?" "Of course not, Bertie. Now go put your shoes in the garage, the dinner is ready

497. Two cannibals are enjoying dinner. One compliments the other, "I say, Bill, your wife really makes a great meal."

498. Two Arabs sit in the Gaza Strip, enjoying a quiet pint of goat milk. One takes out his wallet and starts flipping through the pictures. - "This is my oldest son. He's a martyr. This here is my second son. He's also a martyr!" - The second Arab nods, "They blow up so fast, don't they?"

499. Three kids are at a Zoo. They seem to be fighting near a wolf enclosure so an adult walks up to them and asks them their names and what they're up to. The first kid says his name is Ronnie and that he was simply trying to feed pickles to the wolves. The second kid introduces herself as Libby and says she was also just trying

to feed pickles to the wolves. The third child introduces herself as Pickles.

Jokes 500 - 549

500. There's no way you're going out in this skirt, kiddo!" - "But mom, I've got great legs, why should I hide them?!" - "Because it's so short and your nuts are showing underneath!"

501. Jokes about PMS are NOT funny. Period.

502. A guy walks into a pharmacy: "I have extreme headaches, my belly cramps, I feel like I'm about to vomit and my back hurts like something tears the muscles apart. Do you have something?" - Pharmacists: "Nope, I feel fine."

503. I've seen this show about beavers last night – best dam documentary I've ever seen!"

504. I have the memory of an elephant. - I very clearly remember seeing an elephant once in the Chicago zoo.

505. Are you two twins? No, why do you ask? Because mommy dressed you both in the same clothes. OK that's enough, your driver's license please.

506. "Mom, don't get alarmed, but I'm at the hospital." "Son, please. You've been a surgeon there for 8 years now. Can we start our phone calls differently?"

507. What if dogs fetch the ball back only because they think you really like throwing it?

508. A man tells his doctor, "Doc, help me. I'm addicted to Twitter!"
The doctor replies, "Sorry, I don't follow you ...

509. What did the shark say when he ate the clownfish?
This tastes a little funny.

510. What breed of dog can jump higher than buildings?
Any dog, because buildings can't jump.

511. I have a fear of speed bumps.
But I am slowly getting over it.

512. A plateau is the highest form of flattery.

513. What's a foot long and slippery? A slipper!

514. What do you call bears with no ears? B.

515. My girlfriend treats me like God. She ignores my existence and only talks to me when she needs something.

516. I never make mistakes. ...I thought I did once; but I was wrong.

517. A guest is ordering at a restaurant, "Do you think you could bring me what that gentleman over there is having?" - The waiter looks at him sternly, "No sir, I'm very sure he intends to eat it himself."

518. Boy comes up to his father, all angry, "Dad, you remember how you told me to put a potato in my swimming trunks? How you said it would impress the girls?" Father looks up, smiling, "Yeah, did it work?" The boy screams, "You could have

mentioned that the potato goes in the front!"

519. Dentist warns his patient, "This might be a bit painful." Patient: "That's OK, I'll handle it." The dentist sighs, "For a while now, I've been having an affair with your wife."

520. A wife goes to consult a psychiatrist about her husband: "My husband is acting so weird. He drinks his morning coffee and then he goes and eats the mug! He only leaves the handle!" Psychiatrist: "Yes, that is weird. The handle is the best part."

521. "Daddy, what is an alcoholic?" - "Do you see those 4 trees, son? An alcoholic would see 8 trees." - "Um, Dad – there are only 2 trees."

522. The inventor of AutoCorrect is a stupid mass hole. He can fake right off.

523. Two guys are out hunting in the woods when one of them collapses. He doesn't appear to be breathing, his eyes are glazed over. The other man pulls out his phone with trembling fingers and calls 911. He gasps, "My friend is dead! What can I do?"

The operator says "Please stay calm. I will help you. First of all, let's make sure he's dead."   There's a silence, then a gunshot. The guy gets back on the phone and says "OK, now what?"

524. "I really don't know which kid I'm supposedly being unfair to, according to my wife, Thomas, Anton, or the fat, ugly one?"

525. I was walking past a clothes shop and saw a beautiful dress in the shop window. I went in and asked the shop assistant, "Hi, can I please try on the dress in the shop window?" "Of course," nodded the shop assistant, "but you know we also have changing rooms, right?"

526. The guy who gives out food at the prison canteen asks: "Eat here or take away?" - The prisoner frowns: "Not funny, Marlon! Not funny at all!!"

527. When I drink coffee I can't sleep. – Really? I have the exact opposite. – Wow, seriously? – Yes, when I sleep I can't drink coffee.

528. A mother asks her son, "Paul, would you say I'm pretty or ugly?" - "A bit of both, actually," replies the teenager. - "How do you mean that?" asks the mother. - "I'd say you're pretty ugly."

529. Don't you hate it when you come to somebody's place and they just can't shut up asking you stupid questions like "what do you want" and "who are you"

530. Man to the shop assistant: "I'll have that thing there, please." Shop assistant: "Cupcake?" Man: "OK, Cupcake, I'll have that thing there, please."

531. I spent half an hour trying to take off my girlfriend's bra. I gave up at the end. I wish I never tried it on in the first place.

532. He: "I work with animals every day!"
She: "Oh how sweet! What is it that you do?"
He: "I'm a butcher."

533. "Mommy, there's something wrong with the bunny..." - "Shush, child, please leave the oven door closed." A message for the

534. Doctor: "Do you do sports?" Patient:
"Does sex count?" Doctor: "Yes." Patient:
"Then no."

535. There was a man who entered a local
paper's pun contest.
He sent in ten different puns, in the hope
that at least one of the puns would win.
Unfortunately, no pun in ten did.

536. Yesterday I accidentally sent a naked
picture of myself to everyone in my
address book.
Not only was it embarrassing but it cost a
fortune in stamps.

537. What's the difference between a flying pig
and a politician?
The letter F.

538. I love what you've done with your hair.
How do you get it to come out of the
nostrils like that?

539. A man goes to the doctor with a carrot up
his nose, and a parsnip in his ear,
the doc said, "clearly you're not eating
properly."

540. I really need to confront my phobia of German sausages, but I fear the wurst.

541. Did you hear about the cross-eyed teacher?
He couldn't control his pupils.

542. Doctor, Doctor I think I need glasses.
You certainly do, Sir, this is a fish and chip shop !

543. The new employee stood before the paper shredder looking confused.
"Need some help?" a secretary asked.
"Yes," he replied. "How does this thing work?"
"Simple," she said, taking the fat report from his hand and feeding it into the shredder.
"Thanks, but where do the copies come out?"

544. As the doctor completed an examination of the patient, he said, "I can't find a cause for your complaint. Frankly, I think it's due to drinking."
"In that case," said the patient, "I'll come back when you're sober."

545. How can you tell when you've run out of invisible ink?

546. What do you call a monkey with a banana in each ear?
Anything you want, it can't hear you!

547. Wife: "What are you doing?"
Husband: Nothing.
Wife: "Nothing? You've been reading our marriage certificate for an hour.
Husband: "I was looking for the expiration date."

548. Patient - Doctor doctor! I feel like a dog.
Doctor - How long have you felt like this?
Patient - Since I was a puppy.

549. Unlike milk, it's okay to cry over spilled wine!

550. A recent worldwide survey showed that out of 2,146,703,436 people, 94% were too lazy to actually read that number.

551. Duck walks up to the road. Looks both ways and starts to cross. Chicken standing

near him says, "Dude, you will never hear the end of this."

552. Whatever you do in life, always give 100%. Unless you're donating blood.

553. While visiting a country school, the chairman of the Board Of Education became provoked at the noise the unruly students were making in the next room. Angrily, he opened the door and grabbed one of the taller boys who seemed to be doing most of the talking. He dragged the boy to the next room and stood him in the corner.
A few minutes later, a small boy stuck his head in the room and pleaded, "Please, sir, may we have our teacher back?"

554. For his birthday I gave my son an iPhone. My daughter received an iPod for hers, and for my birthday I was pleased to receive an iPad.
Thinking along the same lines, I got my wife an iRon, and that's when the fight started...

555. Patient goes to Doctor, doctor starts looking at him...

- Good, good, good...
- Doctor, what's good?
- Good that I don't have what you have...

556. I'd like to have more self-esteem, but I
don't deserve it.

557. 'What kind of work do you do?' a woman
passenger enquired of the man travelling
in her train compartment.
'I'm a Naval surgeon,' he replies.
'My word!' spluttered the woman, 'How
you doctors specialise these days.'

558. What's the difference between a bad
golfer and a bad skydiver?
A bad golfer goes WHACK! ... "Darn".
A bad skydiver goes "Darn" ... WHACK!

559. A drunk in a bar is yelling "All lawyers are
thieves"
The guy sitting next to him says, "Whoa,
easy there buddy."
The drunk says, "Are you a lawyer?"
"No, I'm a thief", he replied.

560. I just got a new job as a security guard.
My boss told me that my main job is to
watch the office.

I'm on season 4 so far, but I'm not sure what this has to do with security.

561. We were so poor when I was growing up we couldn't even afford to pay attention.

562. The three stages of sex in marriage: tri-weekly, try-weekly, and try-weakly.

563. My inferiority complex isn't as good as everyone else's.

564. A saw and a hammer go into a bar and some other tools join them; the saw turns to the hammer and says 'You know the drill, don't you?'

565. Son: 'Dad, can I go to the bathroom?' ~ Dad: 'MAY I go to the bathroom?' ~ Son: 'But I asked first!'

566. I wanted to marry my English teacher when she got out of jail, but apparently you can't end a sentence with a proposition.

567. An English teacher wrote these words on the whiteboard: "woman without her man

is nothing".
The teacher then asked the students to punctuate the words correctly.
The men wrote: "Woman, without her man, is nothing."
The women wrote: "Woman! Without her, man is nothing."

568. My wife and I decided not to have kids.
The kids are taking it pretty badly.

569. I bought my wife a Pug as a present.
Despite the squashed nose, bulging eyes and rolls of fat, the dog seems to like her.

570. I made a graph of all my past relationships.
It has an ex axis and a why axis.

571. A married couple is sleeping when the phone rings at 3 AM.
The wife picks up the phone and, after a few seconds, replies, "How am I supposed to know? We're 200 miles inland!" and hangs up.
Her husband rolls over and asks, "Sweetheart, who was that?"
"I don't know, some dumb blonde asking if the coast is clear."

572. I am single by choice.
A choice made by those reluctant to date me.

573. I have a pen that can actually write underwater!
It can also write other words too.

574. "Berni asks her father: 'Dad, what does a football player do when he can't see very well anymore?
Dad: 'He becomes a referee!'"

575. My sister asked for me to bring her something hard to write on.
I don't know why she got so mad at me. It is pretty hard to write on sand.

576. Why do women fake orgasms?
Because they want to give men the impression that they have climaxed.

577. What do you say to a woman with two black eyes?
"Would you like an ice pack?"

578. A man went to visit a friend and was amazed to find him playing chess with his

dog.

He watched the game in astonishment for a while.

"I can hardly believe my eyes!" he exclaimed. "That's the smartest dog I've ever seen."

"Nah, he's not so smart," the friend replied. "I've beaten him three games out of five."

579. What is the tallest building in the world? The library! It has the most stories!

580. Two campers are walking through the woods when a huge brown bear suddenly appears in the clearing about 50 feet in front of them.

The bear sees the campers and begins to head toward them.

The first guy drops his backpack, digs out a pair of sneakers, and frantically begins to put them on.

The second guy says, "What are you doing? Sneakers won't help you outrun that bear."

"I don't need to outrun the bear," the first guy says, "I just need to outrun you."

581. What's the different between a cat and a comma?
A cat has claws at the end of paws; A comma is a pause at the end of a clause.

582. What do you call a priest who becomes a lawyer?
A father in law.

583. A Lady to Doctor: "My husband has a habit of talking in his sleep! what should I give him"?
Doctor: Give him an Opportunity to speak when he's awake.

584. Spotting the befuddled CEO holding a piece of paper and standing by the shredder, the assistant decided to help. "This document's very important," said the CEO. "Can you make this thing work?"The assistant turned the machine on, inserted the paper, and pressed "start.""Great," said the CEO as his paper disappeared into the machine. "I just need one copy."

585. My wife asked if she could have a little peace and quiet while she cooked dinner. I said sure and took the batteries out of the smoke detector.

586. "Which book has helped you the most in your life?"
"My father's check book!"

587. A father came home from a long business trip to find his son riding a new 21 speed mountain bike.
"Where did you get the money for the bike? It must have cost $300," he asked.
"Easy, Dad," little Johnny replied. "I earned it hiking."
"Come on Johnny," the father said. "Tell me the truth."
"That is the truth!" Johnny replied.
"Every night you were gone, Mom's boss, Mr. Reynolds, would come over to see Mom. He'd give me a $20 bill and tell me to take a hike!"

588. Scientists have discovered another deadly pathogen they are calling the Peekaboo virus. Doctors are sending anyone with peekaboo straight to ICU.

589. A psychiatrist was testing a patient's personality. He drew a circle on a paper. And asked the patient, "What does this remind you of?"
The patient answered, "Sex."

The shrink drew a square and asked again,
"What does this remind you of?"
"Sex," the patient replied.
Then the doctor drew a triangle.
"It reminds me of sex," the patient stated.
"You seem to be obsessed with sex," the
shrink told the patient.
"I'm obsessed with sex? You're the one
who's drawing the dirty pictures!"

590. I'm American, and I'm sick of people
saying America is "the stupidest country in
the world."
Personally, I think Europe is the stupidest
country in the world.

591. What's the difference between a good
secretary and a personal secretary?
One says "Good morning, boss !".
The other says " It's morning, boss !"

592. I work in China with a guy named Kim
One day we were drinking and I asked him
if he's fed up of westerns saying that all
Chinese look the same.
He said "Kim's at the bar getting drinks I'm
his wife"

593. A man and a friend are playing golf one day at their local golf course. One of the guys is about to chip onto the green when he sees a long funeral procession on the road next to the course.

He stops in mid-swing, takes off his golf cap, closes his eyes, and bows down in prayer.

His friend says: "Wow that is the most thoughtful and touching thing I have ever seen. You truly are a kind man."

The man then replies: "Yeah, well we were married 35 years."

594. One student fell into a cycle of classes, studying, working and sleeping.

Didn't realise how long he had neglected writing home until he received the following note:

"Dear Son, Your mother and I enjoyed your last letter.

Of course, we were much younger then... and more impressionable.

Love, Dad."

595. A man had six children and was very proud of his achievement.

He was so proud of himself that he started calling his wife, 'Mother of Six', in spite of her objections.

One night they went to a party. He decided that it was time to go home, and wanted to find out if his wife is ready to leave as well.

He shouted at the top of his voice, "Shall we go home, Mother of Six?"

His wife, irritated by her husband's lack of discretion shouted back, "Anytime you're ready, Father of Four!"

596. Policeman: Why are you driving without a license?

Motorist: Because it was revoked months ago.

597. What can coronavirus do that the United States government can't?

Stop school shootings.

598. Build a man a fire and he'll be warm for one night.

Set a man on fire and he'll be warm for the rest of his life.

599. When I see two lovers' names carved in a tree, I don't think its romantic.

I just think it's really strange how many people bring knives on a date.

600. A little boy, at a wedding looks at his mom and says, "Mommy, why does the girl wear white?" His mom replies, "The bride is in white because she's happy and this is the happiest day of her life." The boy thinks about this, and then says, "Well then, why is the boy wearing black?"

601. What's the difference between a musician and a large pizza?
A large pizza can feed a family of four.

602. A recent survey was conducted to discover why men get out of bed in the middle of the night:
- 5% said it was to get a glass of water.
- 12% said it was to go to the toilet.
- 83% said it was to go home.

603. Dad can you explain to me what a solar eclipse is?
No sun.

604. What do you call a psychic midget who has escaped from prison?
A small medium at large.

605. What did the psychiatrist say to the naked man?
Well, I can clearly see your nuts.

606. "De Beers" and "the beers" are both very costly, and both can sometimes get similar results from your girlfriend.

607. I bought a new deodorant stick today. The instructions read: REMOVE WRAPPER AND PUSH UP THE BOTTOM PART." I can hardly walk now, but whenever I fart, the room smells divine.

608. I heard something this morning that really made me open my eyes.
What was it?
My alarm clock.

609. Man: "Little girl, I'm looking for a small black and white dog with only one eye."
Little Girl: "If he's small, perhaps you should use both eyes.

610. While ferrying workers back and forth from our offshore oil rig, the helicopter I was on lost power and went down. Fortunately, it landed safely in a lake. Struggling to get out, one man tore off his

seat belt, inflated his life vest and jerked open the exit door.

"Don't jump!" the pilot called out. "This thing is supposed to float!"

As the man leapt from the helicopter into the lake, he yelled back, "Yeah, and it's supposed to fly too!"

611. Teacher: "What is the chemical formula for water?"
Student: "HIJKLMNO."
Teacher: "What are you talking about?"
Student: "Yesterday you said it's H to O!"

612. A professor was giving a big test one day to his students. He handed out all of the tests and went back to his desk to wait. Once the test was over the students all handed the tests back in. The professor noticed that one of the students had attached a $100 bill to his test with a note saying "A dollar per point."
The next class the professor handed the graded tests back out. This student got back his test, his test grade, and $64 change.

613. Bob: "Holy crap, I just fell off a 50 ft ladder."

Jim: "Oh my God, are you okay?"
Bob: "Yeah it's a good thing I fell off the first step."

614. What starts with E, ends with E, and has only 1 letter in it?
Envelope.

615. Little Johnny is always being teased by the other neighbourhood boys for being stupid.
Their favourite joke is to offer Johnny his choice between a nickel and a dime Little Johnny always takes the nickel.
One day, after Johnny takes the nickel, a neighbour takes him aside and says, "Johnny, those boys are making fun of you. Don't you know that a dime is worth more than a nickel, even though the nickel's bigger?"
Johnny grins and says, "Well, if I took the dime, they'd stop doing it, and so far I've made $20!"

616. If I had a dollar for every time a woman found me unattractive, eventually they would start to find me attractive.

617. A woman who lived next door to a preacher was puzzled by his personality change. At home he was shy, quiet and retiring, but in the church he was a real fire orator, rousing the masses in the name of God. It was as if he were two different people.

One day she asked him about the dramatic transformation that came over him when he preached.

"Ah," he said, "That's my altar ego."

618. I'm American, and I'm sick of people saying America is "the stupidest country in the world."

Personally, I think Europe is the stupidest country in the world.

619. What starts with a P, ends with an E, and has a million letters in it?

Post Office!

620. I'm so bored that I just memorized six pages of the dictionary.

I learned next to nothing.

621. What's the difference between a good secretary and a personal secretary?

One says "Good morning, boss !".
The other says " It's morning, boss !"

622. A policeman comes to the office with one black shoe and one white shoe. His boss starts to yell at him:
- You are ruining police reputation, go home and change the shoes.
The policeman goes home, and comes back after a while.
- Boss I have a problem, the other pair of shoes at home are black and white, too.

623. What's the difference between a hippo and a Zippo? One's really heavy, the other's a little lighter.

624. Little Johnny attended a horse auction with his father.
He watched as his father moved from horse to horse, running his hands up and down the horse's legs, rump and chest.
After a few minutes, Johnny asked, "Dad, why are you doing that?"
His father replied, "Because when I'm buying horses, I have to make sure that they are healthy and in good shape before I buy."

Johnny, looking worried said, "Dad, I think the FedEx guy wants to buy Mom."

625. What dog keeps the best time?
A watch dog.

626. At the doctor's office, Tom was getting a check up. "I have good news and bad news," says the doctor. "The good news is you have 24 hours left to live." Tom replies, "That's the good news?!" Then the doctor says, "The bad news is I should have told you that yesterday."

627. A congressional aide asks the politician, "What should we do about this abortion bill?"
Politician: Shh. Just pay it.

628. A young boy came home from school and told his mother, "I had a big fight with my classmate.
He called me a sissy." The mother asked, "What did you do?"
The boy replied, "I hit him with my purse!"

629. What's easy to get into, but hard to get out of?
Trouble.

630. I'm waiting for the day that scientists discover a cure for Natural Causes.

631. Last night I got a little drunk at a bar so I decided to take the bus home. Good thing I did because there was a sobriety checkpoint on the way. The police just waved the bus through and I got home safely.
    Until yesterday I had no idea I could drive a bus, but I'm pretty good at it if you ask me.

632. What is the definition of a last will and testament?
    You should know the answer, it is a dead giveaway.

633. A man called his child's doctor, "Hello! My son just snatched my pen when I was writing and swallowed it.
    What should I do?" The doctor replied, "Until I can come over, write with another pen."

634. A husband and wife had four boys. The odd part of it was that the older three had red hair, light skin, and were tall, while the youngest son had black hair, dark eyes,

117

and was short.

The father eventually took ill and was lying on his deathbed when he turned to his wife and said, "Honey, before I die, be totally honest with me – is our youngest son my child?"

The wife replied, "I swear on everything that's holy that he is your son."

With that the husband passed away. The wife then muttered, "Thank God he didn't ask about the other three."

635. I had a fear of speed bumps, but I'm slowly getting over it.

636. 6 out of 7 dwarfs aren't Happy.

637. What would bears be without bees?
Ears.

638. What's the difference between roast beef and pea soup?
Anyone can roast beef.

639. Sam: Hey John!
John: Hey!
Sam: Did you know Microsoft just bought Skype for ten million dollars?
John: Really!?

John: Idiots.... They could have downloaded it for free.

640. A lawyer and a regular average Joe are on a plane together. The pilot comes on the speaker and announces that the flight will take up to 16 hours. The lawyer turns to Joe and says, "Okay, I have a game we can play while we pass the time. You ask me any question, and if I can't answer it, I'll give you $50. Then, I get to ask you a question, any question, and if you can't answer it, you give me $5." The average Joe says, "Okay, what has four legs going up a hill, and three legs at the bottom?" The lawyer thinks for a moment, then hands Joe $50 and says, "Wow, that was tough. I don't know, what does have four legs going up a hill and three legs at the bottom?" Joe then hands the lawyer $5 and says to him, "There's your $5."

641. Frank was getting ready to go on a trip to New York for the first time, and was talking to his friend Bill.
Bill: "While you are in New York, there is a bar that you have to go to. When you walk through the front door, you are handed a free drink. Then you can go to the back

room and get laid. Come back up to the bar, and you get another free drink. Then you can get laid again. It goes on like this all night."

Frank: "That sounds unbelievable. Have you really been there?"

Bill: "No, but my sister has."

642. "Johnny, why did you kick your brother in the stomach?" exclaimed the angry mother.

"It was pure accident, Mama. He turned around."

643. Did you hear about the guy who's whole left side was cut off?
He's all right now.

644. Police arrested two kids yesterday, one was drinking battery acid, the other was eating fireworks. They charged one – and let the other one off.

645. An Essex girl was driving down the A13 when her car phone rang.
It was her boyfriend, urgently warning her, "Treacle, I just heard on the news that there's a car going the wrong way on the A13. Please be careful!"

"It's not just one car!" said the Essex girl, "There are hundreds of them!"

646. How many politicians does it take to change a light bulb?
Two: one to change it and another one to change it back again.

647. Confucius: Man who want pretty nurse, must be patient.

648. Jill: You remind me of the sea.
Jack: Because I'm wild, unpredictable and romantic?
Jill: No, because you make me sick.

649. Casey married a rich widow, but they didn't get along.
One day she said to him, "If it wasn't for my money, that new television wouldn't be here.
If it wasn't for my money, that grand piano wouldn't be here.
If it wasn't for my money, this house wouldn't be here."
Casey mumbled, "If it wasn't for your money, I wouldn't be here."

650. My wife asked me to buy ORGANIC vegetables from the market. I went and looked around and couldn't find any.
So I grabbed an old, tired looking employee and said, "These vegetables are for my wife. Have they been sprayed with any poisonous chemicals?"
"The produce guy looked at me and said, "No. You'll have to do that yourself."

651. Why wouldn't the shrimp share his treasure?
Because he was a little shellfish.

652. What's the easiest way to remember your wife's birthday?
Forget it once!

653. Why does a barber never shave a man with a wooden leg?
Because he always uses a razor.

654. A doctor examining a woman who had been rushed to A&E, took the husband aside, and said, 'I don't like the looks of your wife at all.
Me neither doc, said the husband, but she's a great cook and really good with the kids.

655. A child goes to a baptism with his parents and, as the priest dipped the baby's head into the font, asked them "Why is that man brain-washing that baby?"

656. When i was younger all the other kids used to push me around and call me lazy. I miss that wheelchair.

657. A man was passing a country estate and saw a sign on the gate. It read: "Please ring bell for the caretaker."
   He rang the bell and an old man appeared.
   "Are you the caretaker?" the fellow asked.
   "Yes, I am," replied the old man. "What do you want?"
   "I'd just like to know why you can't ring the bell yourself."

658. An old lady owned two monkeys.
   One day they both died, so she took them to the taxidermist."So you want them mounted?" asked the taxidermist.
   To which she replied: "No. Holding hands will do just fine."

659. I've never understood why women love cats.

Cats are independent, they don't listen,
they don't come in when you call them,
they like to stay out all night, come home
and expect to be fed and stroked, then
want to be left alone and sleep
In other words, every quality that women
hate in a man, they love in a cat.

660. Conversation in the immigration office at
airport in the US:
– Your name, Sir.
– Bakshish Abdul
– Sex
– Three times a day...
– I mean male or female?
– Doesn't matter.

661. Two male flies are buzzing around,
cruising for good looking females.
One spots a real cutie sitting on a pile of
cow dung and dives down toward
her."Pardon me" he asks, turning on his
best charm,"...but is this stool taken?"

662. One day Mongo is in his back yard digging
a hole. His neighbour, seeing him there,
decides to investigate."What are you
doing?" he asked.
Mongo replies, "My goldfish died and I'm

burying him.""That's an awful big hole for a goldfish, isn't it?" asked the neighbour. Mongo shot back, "that's because he's inside your f***** cat!"

663. What do you get when you breed a Bulldog and a Shitzu together? A Bullshit.

664. A man running a little behind schedule arrives at a picture theatre.
He goes in to watch the movie that has already started, and as his eyes adjust to the darkness, he is surprised to see a dog sitting beside its master in the row ahead, intently watching the movie.
It even seemed to be enjoying the movie: wagging its tail in the happy bits, drooping its ears at the sad bits, and hiding its eyes with its paws at the scary bits.
After the movie, the man approaches the dog's owner," Jeez mate, your dog really seemed to enjoy the movie. I'm amazed!"
"Yes, I'm amazed also," came the reply.
"He hated the book."

665. Wife comes back from the doctor and says to her husband:
"Honey, I have a sad news – a gynaecologist told me not have sex for a

three weeks."

Husband: "and what the dentist said?"

666. "What's the difference between the North
American porcupine and the African
porcupine," the society matron asked the
zookeeper."
The principal difference is the North
American species has a longer prick."
This, as you might assume, distressed the
matron who stormed immediately to the
zoo manager's office. The zoo manager
said, "Ma'am, I apologize for my staff's
unfortunate choice of terms.
What the keeper should have said is the
North American species has a longer quill.
In fact, their pricks are just about the same
size."

667. A robber was robbing a house when he
heard a voice. "Jesus is watching you!"
"Who's there?" The robber said, but no
sound was heard. So he kept going and he
heard it two more times when he spotted
a parrot.
"What's your name," the robber asked the
parrot. "Cocodora" said the parrot. "Now,
what kind of idiot would name a bird
Cocodora" said the robber.

"The same idiot who named the Rottweiler Jesus", said the parrot.

668. My credit card was stolen but I'm not sure if I should report it.
The thief is spending a lot less than my wife normally does.

669. I wish that there was a restaurant named "I don't care" so I'd finally know where my girlfriend was talking about.

670. There are four people named Everybody, Somebody, Anybody and Nobody.
There was an important job to be done and Everybody was asked to do it.
Everybody was sure Somebody would do it.
Anybody could have done it, but Nobody did it. Somebody got angry about that, because it was Everybody's job.

671. If con is the opposite of pro, does that mean Congress is the opposite of progress?

672. Why is it so hard for women to find men that are sensitive, caring, and good-looking?

Because those men already have boyfriends.

673. A man and his blonde wife are lying in bed trying to sleep but the neighbour's dog won't stop barking.
The blonde decides she has had enough. She jumps out of bed and says, "I'm not going to listen to that dog bark all night in the neighbour's backyard". She goes downstairs and after several minutes she returns to bed.
When she gets to bed the husband says, "Honey, the dog is still barking, what did you do down there?". The blonde replies, "I put the dog in our backyard, let's see how they like it!"

674. I like my women like I like my coffee.
From a third world country and at a reasonable price.

675. I went by the house where I grew up in yesterday.
I asked to go in to look around, but they said no and shut the door in my face.
My parents can be so mean sometimes.

676. I took my three year old son to the mall yesterday. When we got home, I noticed that he had a chocolate bar in his pocket. Now, I know I didn't buy it and he certainly didn't buy it.
So I marched him straight back to the mall and took him to the jewellers.

677. I say no to alcohol, it just doesn't listen.

678. I was at a climbing centre the other day, but someone had stolen all the grips from the wall.
You couldn't make it up!

679. Apparently someone gets stabbed in London every 52 seconds.
If I was them I would move.

680. A little girl and boy are fighting about the differences between the sexes, and which one is better. Finally, the boy drops his pants and says, "Here's something I have that you'll never have!" The little girl is pretty upset by this, since it is clearly true, and runs home crying. A while later, she comes running back with a smile on her face. She drops her pants and says, "My

mommy says that with one of these, I can have as many of those as I want!"

681. Your village called...
They want their idiot back.

682. Why isn't there mouse-flavoured cat food?

683. Why are they called apartments when they are all stuck together?

684. My new girlfriend works at the zoo. I think she's a keeper.

685. A woman was in the kitchen doing the boiled eggs for breakfast. Her husband walks in and she says, "You've got to make love to me this very moment."
The husband, thinking it's his lucky day, makes love to her on the kitchen table. Afterward he says, "What was that all about?"
She says, "The egg timer's broken...........

686. The wife to the husband: Tomorrow is our 20 years anniversary, can we cook the pig?
Why? It's not his fault.

687. A bit of rope walks in to a bar, the barman say "Are you a bit of rope? We don't serve rope here"
The rope replies "No I'm afraid not"

688. Little Sally came home from school with a smile on her face, and told her mother, "Frankie Brown showed me his weenie today at the playground!" Before the mother could raise a concern, Sally went on to say, "It reminded me of a peanut." Relaxing with a hidden smile, Sally's mom asked, "Really small, was it?" Sally replied, "No, salty." Mom fainted.

689. Unexpected sex – that's a great way to wake up.
If you are not in a prison.

690. When I was in the pub I heard a couple of chaps saying that they wouldn't feel safe on an aircraft if they knew the pilot was a woman.
What a pair of sexist pigs. I mean, it's not as if she'd have to reverse the bloody thing.

691. A study recently concluded that licking the sweat from frogs can cure depression.

The bad news is that when you stop licking the frog gets depressed again.

692. I saw a guy stacking shelves at the supermarket complaining because the top shelf was broken, and he couldn't keep it up. I think he had A wrecked aisle dysfunction.

693. Four friends are touring Europe. One is English, one is French, another is Spanish, and the last is from Germany.
The four friends are in Paris, and see a large crowd gathering around a street performer.
They all crane their necks to see the street performer, but can't seem to get a view.
The performer notices the men, and stands on a box. He yells out "Can you gents in the back see me alright?"
The friends respond: Yes, Oui, Si, Ja.

694. "A man and his wife were having a big argument at breakfast. He shouted at her, "You aren't so good in bed either!" Then stormed off to work.
By mid-morning, he decided he'd better make amends and called home. "What took you so long to answer?" he asked.

"I was in bed," she replied.
"What were you doing in bed this late?"
"Getting a second opinion."

695.   What is a similarity between a pregnant
       14-year-old and the fetus inside of her?
       They both are thinking "Shit! Mom is going
       to kill me!"

696.   The next sentence is telling the truth. The
       previous sentence is telling a lie.

697.   My poor knowledge of Greek mythology
       has always been my Achilles' elbow.

698.   A feminist asked me how I view lesbian
       relationships.
       Apparently "in HD" wasn't a good
       answer☐.

699.   I had to clean out my spice rack and found
       everything was too old and had to be
       thrown out. – What a waste of thyme.

700.   Why don't blind people skydive? –
       Because it scares their dogs too much!

701. What is the second hardest thing in the morning?
Getting up.

702. What's the difference between America and a bottle of milk? – In 200 years the milk will have developed a culture.

703. Why can't humans hear a dog whistle? – Because dogs can't whistle.

704. Welcome back to the hide and seek world championship! Osama Bin Laden vs. Anne Frank!

705. Why can't they blonde call 911
Can she can't find the 11

706. Roses are red, violets are blue, You think violets are blue, what the hell is wrong with you.

707. What's the best part of dating a homeless girl?
You can drop her off anywhere.

708. why are dolphins so smart? Because within three hours they can train a human

to stand at the edge of the pool and feed them fish!

709. I think my co-workers are gay. – Every time I walk by, they mumble, "What an ass."

710. What's the difference between people and chocolate? I can still buy dark chocolate

711. My girlfriend broke up with me. She said I was a paedophile. I replied, "paedophile? Wow, that sure is a big word for an eight-year-old!"

712. For sale: Dead Canary.
Not going cheep.

713. Son: Dad am I adopted? Father: What? No! Out of all the kids in the adoption centre do you really think I would pick u?

714. How many kids does it take to change a light bulb well it's not 53 cause my basements still dark

715. I tried to explain to my 4 year old son that it's perfectly normal to accidentally poop your pants. – But he's still making fun of me.

716. Why do women have cleaner minds than men? – Because they change theirs more often.

717. What do you call a cross between a gorilla and a monkey? – A cross.

718. My wife left me for an Indian guy. – I know he's going to treat her well, I heard they worship cows.

719. What do you call a catholic priest who molests children? A catholic priest

720. My bank loves me.
They told me my credit card balance is outstanding.
If sex with three people is called a threesome and sex with four people is called a foursome, I guess now it's clear why everyone calls me handsome.

721. Oh you're talking to me, I thought you only talked behind my back.

722. After God created 24 hours of alternating darkness and light, one of the angels asked him, "What are you going to do now?"
God said, "I think I'm going to call it a day."

723. Sherlock Holmes and Dr. Watson decide to go on a camping trip. After dinner and a bottle of wine, they lay down for the night, and go to sleep.
Some hours later, Holmes awoke and nudged his faithful friend.
"Watson, look up at the sky and tell me what you see."
Watson replied, "I see millions of stars."
"What does that tell you?"
Watson pondered for a minute.
"Astronomically, it tells me that there are millions of galaxies and potentially billions of planets." "Astrologically, I observe that Saturn is in Leo." "Horologically, I deduce that the time is approximately a quarter past three." "Theologically, I can see that God is all powerful and that we are small and insignificant." "Meteorologically, I

suspect that we will have a beautiful day tomorrow." "What does it tell you, Holmes?"

Holmes was silent for a minute, then spoke: "Watson, you idiot. Someone has stolen our tent!"

724. The Pope and Donald Trump are on stage in front of a huge crowd.

The Pope leaned towards Trump and said, "Do you know that with one little wave of my hand I can make every person in this crowd go wild with joy? This joy will not be a momentary display, like that of your followers, but go deep into their hearts and for the rest of their lives whenever they speak of this day, they will rejoice!"

Trump replies, "I seriously doubt that. With one little wave of your hand? Show me!"

So the Pope slapped him.

725. A guy wins a free ticket to the Super Bowl and so he's very excited.

However, he's not so excited when he gets there and realizes his seat's in the back of the stadium.

So he looks around him for a better seat, and to his surprise he finds an empty seat right next to the field.

He approaches the older guy who's sitting in the seat next to the empty one and asks if the seat is taken.

The man replies, "No."

The young guy is very surprised to hear this and asks, "How could someone pass up a seat like this?"

The older guy replies, "It's my wife's seat. We've been to every Super Bowl together since the day we were married but she's passed away."

"Oh, how sad," the young guy says, taken aback. "I'm sorry to hear that, but couldn't you find a friend or relative to come with you?"

"No," the man replies, "They're all at the funeral."

726.   One day Nathan came in ten minutes late to Mr Jones's class. Mr Jones asked him, "Nathan, what do you have to say for yourself?" Nathan says, "Please sir, I was on top of Cherry Hill.

Then Dave came in ten minutes later. Mr Jones asked him, "Dave, what do you have to say for yourself?" Dave says, "Please sir, I was on top of Cherry Hill.

Then ten minutes later Mike came in. Mr

Jones asked him, "Mike, what do you have to say for yourself?" Mike says, "Please sir, I was on top of Cherry Hill.

Then five minutes later a new girl walked in to Mr Jones's lesson. Mr Jones is at the end of his tether now and says, "Who are you and why are you late?" The new girl says, "Sir, I'm called Cherry Hill"

727. A elderly woman and an elderly man were at a retirement home The man was shuffling a deck of cards for a card game The man asks "Is it your first time?" The woman replies "It's been a while since a man has asked me that."

728. When Albert Einstein was making the rounds of the speaker's circuit, he usually found himself eagerly longing to get back to his laboratory work. One night as they were driving to yet another rubber-chicken dinner, Einstein mentioned to his driver (a man who somewhat resembled Einstein in looks & manner) that he was tired of speechmaking.

"I have an idea, boss," his driver said. "I've heard you give this speech so many times. I'll bet I could give it for you." Einstein laughed loudly and said, "Why not? Let's do it!"

When they arrived at the dinner, Einstein donned the driver's cap and jacket and sat in the back of the room. The driver gave a beautiful rendition of Einstein's speech and even answered a few questions expertly.

Then a supremely pompous professor asked an extremely esoteric question about anti-matter formation, digressing here and there to let everyone in the audience know that he was nobody's fool. Without missing a beat, the driver fixed the professor with a steely stare and said, "Sir, the answer to that question is so simple that I will let my driver, who is sitting in the back, answer it for me."

729. A priest asks the convicted murderer at the electric chair, "Any last requests?" "Yes," replied the murderer, "Will you please hold my hand?"

730. A drunk man walked out of a bar and kept falling flat on his face. He wondered why this was until his wife spoke to him: Wife: why is your face all bloody? Husband: I was so drunk that I couldn't stand up so I

kept falling on my face! Wife: idiot. You left your wheelchair at the bar!

731. A cop pulls a guy over for suspected drunk driving. The cop opens the door and the driver falls out onto the asphalt. The cop says, "Holy shit, you're so drunk, you can't even walk!"
The drunk says, "No shit, that's why I took my car!"

Printed in Great Britain
by Amazon